Till Only Love Remains

40 Years of Poetry from Robert A. Revel

Written While Listening To Life...

Compiled by Lenni Revel

Forward, Preludes and Afterward by Lenni Revel

COOL TRIBE WORLD® PUBLISHING
Santa Rosa, CA

Copyright © 2018 by Robert A. Revel

All rights reserved. No part of this book may be reproduced or transmitted in any form or by any means, electronic or mechanical, including photocopying, recording, or by any information storage or retrieval system, without permission in writing from the publisher, except by reviewers, who may quote brief passages in a review.

Published by

Cool Tribe World® Publishing
131 A Stony Circle, #500
Santa Rosa, CA 95401

Cover artwork
Lenni Revel

Cover and text design
Caren Parnes, Enterprising Graphics

Editing
Lenni Revel

ISBN 978-1-7322717-3-9

Library of Congress Control Number: 2018909907

Printed in the United States of America

This book is dedicated to all those who struggle with mental illness. When you feel like you're on the edge of everything, the most powerful medicine is the presence of someone who knows that ground intimately, and who somehow managed to come out on the other side a whole person.

-Lenni Revel

Foreword

On a memorable day in January of 2016, a few months after my husband and I moved in together, I went into the garage to look for something. In a crowded corner, an old brown box caught my eye. I walked over to it and instinctively began setting things aside as if to somehow rescue it from the surrounding clutter. I knelt down and decided to open it. Inside I found a neat stack of time worn journals amid a bountiful pile of loose papers.

    I felt my intuition smile. Hungrily, I grabbed the cardboard container and scampered into the house. "Hunny, guess what I found?" He glanced knowingly at what was in my arms. "Ahh, that looks familiar." I put it down and walked over to him, wrapping my arms around his neck. "I'd love to read your journals, if you're okay with it." He pulled me in closer and gently kissed me, and without hesitation replied, "Of course you can read them."

    It took some time, but eventually, I read every journal from cover to cover—an incredible experience that is itself its own story. But that treasure chest was not all I found. I eventually discovered even more time-wilted boxes in the garage, with more heaps of paperwork. I feverishly devoured every scrap of his writings I could get my hands on—at times I felt like an archeologist deciphering crumpled and dog-eared ancient parchment with barely visible scribble. When there was finally

FOREWORD

no more writing to be found, I had managed to unearth over 150 poems written over a 40-year period that my husband had somehow managed not to throw away. The early lyrical offerings, when *not* hand written, were recorded on manual typewriter, before people owned word processing computers. After reading everything, I set out to transcribe every poem and journal entry my soon-to-be husband had written in the last four decades.

Between the chronological bookmarkers of 1976 and 2016, an extraordinary story unfolded through his poetry, which I am going to share with you, in addition to a few I have included that he wrote in the years since we have been together. It has been a remarkable experience to become even more connected to this man peering into the many years and stages of his life before we met through his writings—some from more than a decade before I was born. On a personal level, the reverie was very intimate and magical. But I also sensed that I was catching a glimpse of something extraordinary; a rare and deeply subjective look into the life of a soul truly committed to the journey inward—perhaps the fundamental reason why this man had captured my heart. Here was an individual that was passionately navigating the common existential terrain that connects all of us. For most of his life, he privately and diligently catalogued all the exquisite beauty and suffering that proceeds forth from the human condition, along with his excruciating longing to be truly free, genuine and alive.

FOREWORD

In those moments of sitting amid his years of fevered writing, I began to understand how he had developed and evolved into the man I was choosing to marry. Though I know he never intended for these writings to ever be seen publicly, I feel these insightful musings ought to be made available to others. So eventually I approached him with another question regarding his personal writings… "Would you mind if I published your poetry? I want to share them with the world." He smiled his consent to me as he had done before and said, "Of course they can read them."

Table of Contents

Part One: 1976 to 1985
(Ages 11 to 19)

Part One Prelude 3
Relatively Speaking 5
Playground 6
Silent Tragedy 7
A Friend of the Road 8
Reflections 9
War 10
Riddler's Paradox 11
Paint Them a Picture 13
The Pessimist 14
That Mask 17
Wealth 19
There Is a Face in That Garden 21
A Shoulder 22
Timur Khan 23
Pathway 26
Forgive This Man 28
Where Children Sing 29
Your Part...30
The Inquisition 33
The Chosen...35

TABLE OF CONTENTS

Part Two: 1986 to 1991
(Ages 20 to 25)

Part Two Prelude	39
Not Shackled I, Nor Free	41
When Come Soft Rains	42
For Me?	45
Just Human Beings	46
A Bard's Decree	48
Creation's Fool	50
Big Chill	51
The Edge	53
Monuments, Monoliths, Pyramids and Men	55
The Day Demure	57
Warm Winds	59
Time Drifter	61
Frame In Time	63
Can You Hear?	65
Too Busy Dying	66
Peace	68
I Am	69
Freedom	71
Poor Man's Son	73
Not Yet	74
The Lover	76

TABLE OF CONTENTS

Part Three: 1992 to 1999
(Ages 26 to 33)

Part Three Prelude	79
Message	81
Chains of Fire	82
Darkness	83
The Times We Live In	85
Love That Is Fire	87
Violating The Infinite	89
Plucked	90
Once More?	92
Cycle	95
Emperor of the Grave	96
Conflict Is	98
"Ology's" and "Isms"	99
Nothing to Anyone	100
I Buried You (The Death of Little Self)	101
As Men	104
Dusk To Dawn	106
Eulogy of a Metropolis	107
Another Storm	109
Morning Prayer	110
It Don't Mean Noth'n	111
For Reasons Long Forgotten	113
Sky Poet	115
Where Do You Live	116
Unknown Lover	117

TABLE OF CONTENTS

Part Four: 2000 to 2018
(Ages 34 to 52)

Part Four Prelude	121
My Naked Heart	123
Rising Tide	124
The Journey Forever	125
Ghost Town	126
Home	128
Scattered Matter	130
Woken Up	131
My Teacher	132
I Shall Fight No More Forever	133
Hawk Feather	136
Threshold	138
Enemy, My Enemy	140
Shadows and Shallow Breaths	142
This Dream	143
Repeat Offender	145
Beguiling Lover	146
Mystery	148
No Thought	150
Faith	151
Tete-a-Tete	152
Bring Me to the Fires	154
Meaninglessness	155
Outside Myself	156
Love Completes Itself	158
Hoc Primum Deditionem (This Surrender First)	160

TABLE OF CONTENTS

I Have Never Known	162
Till Only Love Remains	164
What Is Thought?	166
Tonight I Meet the Dragon	168
Beloved	169
A Softness Once	170
My Mother's Son	171
Only Moths	174
The Dreamer	175
I Followed You…	177
Legend	179
No One Hides	181
Lion Heart	183
Afterword	185

PART ONE

Part One
1976 to 1985
(Ages 11 to 19)

PART ONE

PART ONE PRELUDE

In Part One, Robert begins writing at age 11. In these poems it is hard to miss the signs of a young boy who is seeing things rather deeply. So much of what I read in this time period simply fills me with a sense of awe and bewilderment at the interior life of this child. His already penetrating ruminations simmer unnoticed by anyone, just underneath the common routines of a "regular kid." Magically, at this young age, he somehow senses his writings are to be held in trust, and so he privately stashes them away in safe places—an unreasonable habit he would keep for 4 decades until I met him.

In these initial collections I see glimpses of the boy that still lives inside my husband. It is precious and hopeful to imagine us all secreting away the beautiful things we will not allow the world to take from us—to keep them safe in perpetuity. I hope this section inspires in you the same hope, delight, tenderness and appreciation for what can and does move inside our young souls, even in a world where there is not always a place to safely express it.

PART ONE

RELATIVELY SPEAKING
(1976, Age 11. First poem ever written.)

Does the day release the night?
Or do we say it out of spite?
For maybe the night permits the day.
For all is done in a relative way.

Will it rain when the sun goes away?
Or does the sun come out as the rain gives way?
Who are we to even say?
For all is done in a relative way.

Does land halt the seas advance?
Or would land surround water given the chance?
What decides how the world may lay?
For all is done in a relative way.

Who is to claim my words correct,
Philosophy examined, hypotheses checked?
Who am I to even say,
For all is done in a relative way?

PART ONE

PLAYGROUND
(1978, Age 12)

Seasons change, months they are fed,
Until summer rears its ugly head;
Halls empty, students gone,
Only the playground lingers on.

Jingle jangle, playground chains,
Echoes of silence, playground pains;
Whistles of wind through playground bars,
Weathered metal, playground scars.

Swaying pendulum, playground swings,
Concentric circles, playground rings;
Red tree bark, playground floor,
Abused fence gate, playground door.

Waves of children, playground tide,
Lonely structure, playground slide;
Love and joy in children's eyes,
Absence of children, playground dies.

PART ONE

SILENT TRAGEDY
(1979, Age 13)

In the beaming moonlight,
Through the somber fog,
Upon a somnolent bridge,
Near a sleeping dog.

The silhouette of lovers,
Whose time has come and gone,
Whose blossom of love has faded,
As the darkness fades to dawn.

Shall sever all remaining bonds,
And become not friend or foe,
And put it all to rest,
For a reason which neither know.

So in the silence of dying love,
There's nothing left to say,
And as there's two ways off a bridge,
Each go their separate way.

And so ends the tragic love,
But still there creeps the fog,
And through love's wailing pains of death,
Still there sleeps a dog.

PART ONE

A FRIEND OF THE ROAD
(1980, Age 14)

A man can make a friend of the sun
   He can follow it from day to day;
He can sleep at night with the stars above
   And never have much to say.

He can gaze from a cliff and wonder why
   And carry not much of a load;
   Pack up his life in a backpack
   And make a friend of the road.

PART ONE

REFLECTIONS
(1980, Age 14)

Mirror, mirror on the wall,
Are you the reflection of my all?
Is that the real me I see,
Or is it what I appear to be?

Where do I look to see myself,
If not the mirror on the shelf?
Where do I look to see inside,
The likes of which I cannot hide?

All can see who I really am,
But when I look, my vision be damned!
Mirror, mirror can't you see?
You have betrayed the real me.

PART ONE

WAR
(1981, Age 15)

A soldier drinks from a weathered canteen,
Whiskers protruding randomly from his dirt glazed face.

His brow is wet with uncouth perspiration,
As he wipes away the excess moisture on his lips.

He is ready to fight,
       to kill,
             to win.....
                   to die.

But there is no glory in the heat of battle.
No unsung heroes in the tombs of the faceless warriors.

No lingering pride in the faces of the defeated.
No real joy in the faces of the overwhelming victor.

There are no winners,
        or heroes,
          or honor...
            only victims.

PART ONE

RIDDLER'S PARADOX
(1981, Age 15)

Entry to the exit
Close the shut door,
Live in the past
While the past is no more.

Cast a white shadow
Tis the negative sight,
While everything fades
Into white.

Take a step forward
And you'll realize
The future is a product
Of the past's demise.

See what you hear
Taste what you smell,
A warning for the first
The second will tell.

The clocks tick seconds
Each aging the silence,
Decomposing time's visage
Until it is violence.

PART ONE

A man feeds the birds
As they feed him,
Kill the starvation
Kill the loneliness dim.

Words on paper
Trust what they say
Though the author who wrote them
Has led you astray.

PART ONE

PAINT THEM A PICTURE
(1981, Age 15)

Paint them pictures of a glorious battle,
Tell them all how he fought from his saddle.
Tell them all what a hell of a man,
Will fight for his country when he can.

Paint them a picture with colors so bright,
And blind them all from sensible sight.
Let them sign their lives to war,
And once enlisted close the door.

Lock away their heart and soul,
And let the canvas take its toll.
As the portrait takes on a crimson hue,
Let the true colors of the paint show through.

Red for the blood of a million men,
Black for the death of a thousand again,
Green for those who rot in the field,
And clear for the tears that the living must shield.

'Tis a pretty picture you've painted of war,
Brush strokes masking hidden gore,
But for all you war artists, pray I tell,
I hope your paintings burn in hell.

PART ONE

THE PESSIMIST
(1982, Age 16)

The clouds overhead encompass me
The gray hills block my view.
That rock in the road has stubbed my toe
Pleasures in life are few.

This road's too long; it leads nowhere.
Why I walk it, I do not know.
Its very substance grates my feet
If there is beauty, it doesn't show.

The wind it whips my skin till chapped.
It howls in my ears.
It comforts not the blistering heat
And arouses all my fears.

The barren trees, they cast no shade
They stand there as if mute.
Their life is death to those that live
They dare not bear a fruit.

And I am but a particle
Who is cursed to know that he,
Must live a life just for to die,
And that I can't always be.

PART ONE

So trapped am I to live to die
Why live this thing called life?
When every brand new day is cursed
And with it comes more strife.

So beautiful buds are horrid
And the sunshine burns my skin.
And every condemned thought of mine
Is nothing more than sin.

And the future does not promise
The past was never good.
Somehow the present just doesn't
Deliver what it should.

So I question till I'm weary
What's it all about?
Yet nothing more will come to me
Than this disturbing doubt.

Where roads, and hills, and trees, and sun,
Clouds, the wind and life,
The future, past and present
Just cut me like a knife.

PART ONE

The blood it spills into the ground
And no one will ever know,
That here a pessimistic man once stood
Whose thoughts have laid him low.

PART ONE

THAT MASK
(1982, Age 16)

I woke up this morning
Like any other day
But something was different
In a peculiar way.

Was it good or bad?
I could not tell.
I felt strangely exposed,
Coming out of a shell.

What is this feeling?
I began to ask.
I suddenly realized,
I forgot my mask!

You know the mask we all wear?
At night it's on the shelf,
But everyday we put it on,
So as not to expose our self.

You know the game we all play?
The acts we all put on?
Little actors on a stage,
With the audience long since gone.

PART ONE

Well today I lost my script.
And the cues I couldn't see.
And so alone I was forced,
To play the part of me.

So I endured the day,
With my mask upon the shelf.
Living out the frightening experience,
Of just being myself.

But after I had been about it,
It wasn't such a task.
And so just being myself again,
I threw away that mask.

PART ONE

WEALTH
(1982, Age 16)

There once was a man who boasted,
His magnificent wealth be toasted,
"I own land, money, and people too,
I'm filthy rich from hat to shoe."

When from the crowd there arose a sound,
And everybody's head turn 'round.
There among the aristocrats good,
A dirty lowly peasant stood.

There he pointed with finger stout,
Proclaiming: "You are the poorest without a doubt!
I have surpassed your richest high,
For I have seen an eagle fly!

I've heard peasants in the field sing,
And drank the waters of hidden springs.
I've trod my feet through many lands,
And run my fingers through the purest sands.

I've taken breath from tranquil air,
And trusted those you wouldn't dare.
I've risked it all without a care,
And know there's plenty more to share."

PART ONE

And thus he said and did not stir
Waiting upon the mass unsure.
In a moment's time every glass rim
Had taken turn and toasted him.

PART ONE

THERE IS A FACE IN THAT GARDEN
(1982, Age 16)

There is a face in that garden,
Where roses and white lilies grow,
And if there you've ever been,
You'd swear it smiles so.
The fruits grow with such a grin;
Look at the garden! It smiles again!

It seems this garden does possess
In the beauty of its form,
That strange grace and finesse,
Which makes the heart grow warm.
In such beauty can be no sin;
Look at the garden! It smiles again!

Here like eyes the flowers shine,
As soft and rich as skin is soil,
And red as lips grow cherries fine,
With radiant fruits which never spoil.
As fine a face that has ever been;
Look at the garden! It smiles again!

PART ONE

A SHOULDER
(1982, Age 16)

I saw a boy all alone…
Give him a shoulder to cry on.
Thirsting for love right down to the bone,
Give him a shoulder to cry on.

I saw an old man on the park bench…
Give him a shoulder to cry on.
His thirst for a friend has yet been quenched,
Give him a shoulder to cry on.

I saw a poor wino in the gutter…
Give him a shoulder to cry on.
"I am so lonely," I heard him mutter,
Give him a shoulder to cry on.

Let them cry the tears of a thousand fears…
And give them a shoulder to cry on.
Cause maybe some day you will need theirs,
Give them a shoulder to cry on.

PART ONE

TIMUR KHAN
(1982, Age 16)

I've known many a hell of a man in my day,
All have come and gone.
But the hell of a man that went the hardest
Was the man they called Timur Khan.

He stood a towering six foot five,
And three foot wide was he.
Not a single man that challenged him
Ever lived to tell the story.

He never spoke or sung or laughed
But drew carefully each breath.
And the only time he ever smiled
Was in the face of death.

He lived for battle and the smell of blood
Steaming in his nose.
If ever blew a mighty strike
Tis the strike that Timur blows.

As some men walk with dignity
And some men walk with pride,
Timur walked with sword in hand
And all men stepped aside.

PART ONE

'Twas the night before the battle
And the men they reveled on.
But alone and deep in thought
Was the man they called Timur Khan.

In the morning we took to battle
Us and Timur Khan.
As crimson hours flowed like blood
The twilight stole the dawn.

Before we knew it the clash was over
Our enemies had fled.
On the field flowed a river of blood
Which a thousand men had bled.

Amid the men that gave their lives
I did not expect to see,
The man the men called Timur Khan
Down upon one knee.

He knelt regarding his embattled sword,
Took in the bloody rest,
Looked up at the sky, and I swear he smiled…
Then buried his sword in his chest.

PART ONE

No man alive can make the claim
No ogre, troll or elf.
The only hand that could take his life
Was the hand of the Khan himself.

PART ONE

PATHWAY
(1983, Age 17)

From my throne, I sit and rule
And from my throne on high
I see my body is but a tool
For all I rule is I.

I rule me in the daytime
I rule me when I sleep
I rule me when it's playtime
I rule me when I weep.

With the fear of defeat
Comes the need to rule
For fear it would so seem
Is nothing but the fuel.

So I rule me when desires
Give vent to lust and greed.
I rule me when the untruth
Tries to take the lead.

I fight my ego self
And seek with truthful eye,
To distinguish between the truth
And that which is a lie.

PART ONE

And when I am complete
With many battles fought
With those enemies in defeat
I shall have troubles naught.

For when we have no fuel
To furnish all our fears
All the untruth falls away
And reality appears.

Shalt I then be master,
And I shall be content.
Shall I have achieved the purity
For which we all were sent.

PART ONE

FORGIVE THIS MAN
(1984, Age 18)

Forgive this man you see,
For he's frightened deep inside.

He'd really like to love you,
But he only knows to hide.

He doesn't know the mystery
Only that he's scared.

And the sadness overwhelms him
For the heart he never shared.

And he wishes he could cry,
But he knows that he cannot.

Abandoned he his precious soul
And condemned himself to thought.

PART ONE

WHERE CHILDREN SING
(1984, Age 18)

There is a house
Amid a field
Where all the children play.

It once had housed
An affluent man
Now he's passed away.

A grand old palace
To be sure,
The dream of a wealthy eye.

Now vines they feed
Upon the walls,
And weeds they grow so high.

Time devours
Illusions grand,
And laughs at their demise.

While children sing
What a wondrous thing,
That a fool and his money dies.

PART ONE

YOUR PART
(1984, Age 18)

The audience awaits,
The mass anticipates,
The coming of the act
On center stage.

But the actor is afraid,
The play is fear delayed,
And the murmurs of frustration
Border rage.

The player's heart doth pound,
Adding to the sound,
That builds into a
Terrifying noise.

He trembles now backstage,
And fears the public rage,
He knows he must
Confront with austere poise.

No pardon or reprieve,
The public will receive,
What it has paid full price
To come and see.

PART ONE

The actor must perform,
With composure and fine form,
In the last place on earth
He wants to be.

With audience now cheated,
We see history repeated,
As the spotlight shines
On cowardice.

With nothing there to show,
The audience now will go,
And this will be a play
They'll never miss.

The curtains now will close,
No applause or fresh cut rose,
Just the dimming of a spotlight
Once so bright.

Fear has taken away,
The act in someone's play,
Gone forever out of mind
And sight.

And the player...

PART ONE

Despondent and dejected,
Shamed and now rejected,
Bows his head and
Just begins to cry.

But No! In fiery rage,
He steals center stage,
And pulls the curtains
Down once hung high!

Shouts the lines out like a shot,
From a play that's now forgot,
To a waiting audience of
Empty seats.

Like the sounds that no one heard,
A fruitless uttered word,
Fights a battle
That hesitance defeats.

PART ONE

THE INQUISITION
(1984, Age 18)

Someone asked me "Why?" today
I was befuddled, what could I say?

I stood there
Feeling quite amazed,
As if the inquisitor
Was crazed.

When he was sure
I hadn't a clue,
He walked away.
What could he do?

With too much
Time already passed,
The answer came
To me at last!

I ran to catch
Him down the street
So to confess the
Thought complete.

PART ONE

Out of breath
And in a sweat,
Two blocks down
We finally met.

The answer came
Out like a shot,
I looked at him
And said, "Why not?"

I laughed and bellowed
Down the lane.
He must have
Thought me quite insane.

PART ONE

THE CHOSEN
(1985, Age 19)

Sometimes I'll lay in bed at night
And think about this life.
And as I strain
I feel the pain
That cuts me like a knife.

Sometimes I think I hear the rattle
Of a cold and binding chain.
I try to hide
From what's inside,
But still I feel the pain.

Sometimes I fight my very thoughts
And wrestle for control.
I place a bet
On my own sweat,
And hope I get the role.

Sometimes I wonder who I am
And who controls the man.
Should I confide
With who's inside?
I wonder if I can.

PART ONE

When insanity can come and go
As if a desert breeze,
Who is to blame
For why it came,
Or whose mind it may seize?

So I must listen to a silence
A quiet I do not know.
Yet I embrace
Its savings grace
When desert winds do blow.

Shackles on a painted man,
Blood that drips like dew.
And for this test
There is no rest,
Not for the chosen few.

Part Two
1986 to 1991
(Ages 20 to 25)

PART TWO

PART TWO PRELUDE

During this five-year period of Robert's life, something quite significant occurs. I can see expressed in his poetry a young man who is observing the change and impermanence of the exterior world, and it serves to haunt his reveries. The heavy saturation of his emotional body is palpable, and rich with the inevitable sadness, grief, and despair that often accompanies this depth of sensitivity. Yet he seems determined to not only remain rooted in his capacity to endure what he witnesses, but incredibly, to lean into the audacious spectacle of human existence that is so deeply affecting his sensibilities.

Midway through this period, and beginning with the poem "I Am," we can see a soul who is beginning the freshman stages of legitimate introspection and deconstruction of the personal self. Psycho-emotional inventory, soul searching and spiritual accountability all become existential hallmarks of this period—culminating with the amazing poem "The Lover."

As Part Two closes on the conversion of his first quarter of life, we see him approaching a threshold—a radical shift in perspective that brings his orientation of focus from outside to deep within.

PART TWO

NOT SHACKLED I, NOR FREE
(1986, Age 20)

I am the wakeful, watchful one
The bearer of the hour.

I am the noble dutiful knight
Guest in the house of power.

I am a madman like no other
Unleashed in mystery.

I am choice engaged in servitude
Not shackled I, nor free.

PART TWO

WHEN COME SOFT RAINS
(1986, Age 20)

When come soft rains
On window panes
And autumn winds
Are blown.

When tranquil times
Invoke my rhymes
And the seeds of
Heart are sown.

I find a place
Remember a face
And recall some times
Now past.

I feel a fear
And then a tear
And know
It's not the last.

It's you that's real
It's you I feel
Forgive me
If I cheat.

PART TWO

What was so strong
Is now gone long
Yet I see you
So complete.

It's here you stay
Not far away
But deep inside
My mind.

They can't erase
This mental place
Where always
You I find.

And sure enough
When times are rough
I see you
Standing there.

Through the rain
On the window pane
And in
The autumn air.

PART TWO

A smile, a wave
A vision to save
A moment in time
To share.

My name I hear
And a gentle tear
Trickling down
A face so fare.

A whisper's ease
Like an autumn breeze
Is how she
Speaks to me.

A trickling tear
When soft rains appear
Make me
Set her free.

PART TWO

FOR ME?
(1986, Age 20)

Why is it I'm so lonely
Amidst so many friends?
Why do I feel poor
When I've money to lend?

How come I am cold
When the climate is just fine?
Why do I feel lost inside a fog
When the sun does fully shine?

Because I have no one.
Because I am poor at heart.
Because I'm not at home.
Because I am apart.

I find myself in bondage
Where I know I can't be free.
Because everything I ever do
Is only done for me.

PART TWO

JUST HUMAN BEINGS
(1986, Age 20)

Empires eventually crumble
Everything must die
Nothing is invincible
Not them, not you, not I.

No one in this world
Is immune to all the fears
Every man, woman and child
Is susceptible to tears.

There are no eternal heroes
No steadfast tin soldiers true
We are all just human beings
Them like I, like you.

Kings might feel meek
Clowns can sometimes cry
Brave men even worry
Great warriors eventually die.

Don't try to be a superhuman
Cause heroes don't exist
Don't be ashamed to cry a tear
Or in anger clench a fist.

PART TWO

We are all just human beings
Imperfect in the sense
That none of us are flawless
While in our own pretense.

PART TWO

A BARD'S DECREE
(1986, Age 20)

I wrote alone one night
A bard's decree.
Scribbling to the world
Vehemently my testimony.

When then, in a moment
I was observed.
By all that were ever
The greatest of mind.
By all whom had ever
Preached the soul of man.

Attentively they observed,
All without exception.

"Dost thou profess to know
The soul of man?"
The greatest of them spoke to me.

Trembling, I could not even hold my pen.

The inquiry rattled through
The halls of my being.

PART TWO

Speechless and bewildered
I gathered no response.

And then a mighty voice
Rising from the light
Spoke for me.

"Leave the man-child be,
For he is my instrument.
In his hour he knows me.

I am the soul of man.
Do not question my raiment."

PART TWO

CREATION'S FOOL
(1987, Age 21)

Sereneness of silence now broken,
From the echoes of words unspoken.

From the unseen, unknown, and untrue,
Ignore the lies they speak to you.

Mind players, hell sent and bold,
I speak to you, release your hold!

Untruth you speak and games you play,
Go back to the dark and stay away.

Do not cross my path again,
I refuse anymore to feel the pain.

And learn this now that I shall rule,
And you shall play creation's fool.

And suffer so without a cure,
And die even though you never were.

PART TWO

BIG CHILL
(1987, Age 21)

There I sat one day
'Neath a spreading oak
Outside of town
On a rural country road.

I was doing some
Construction work
On a house nearby.
It was this spot I chose for lunch.

My clothes for work
Were old, hardy and dirty—
Best for the trades.
Fancy cars whizzed by.

I must have looked a bum,
For I could clearly see
The fleeting glimpses of pity
In the passing eyes inside those vehicles.

Some of the faces expressed uncertainty,
Probably fear,
Maybe even contempt.
Who can be certain?

PART TWO

My hair was a mess.
My face unshaven.
I seemed a monument
To everything outside their world.

A chilly autumn wind blew
And I wrapped myself tight
In my old, tattered,
Quilted flannel shirt.

God lives in that shirt's material.
For the wind lost its chill
And sought moreover
The vents of the speeding cars.

I could wait here an eternity
And watch the embalmed gaze
Of humans moving too fast to see…

Until they transformed
Into something alive and longing
For an old tattered and torn flannel shirt
To stop the chill.

PART TWO

THE EDGE
(1988, Age 22)

I am old
And I am tired.

With your young and yearning eyes
You beseech me saying,
"Speak old one! Tell me of truths."

And so I say…

Behold the great mirror,
Young one.

And in my eyes
The depths of forever.
For in your own
You cannot see, forever inside you…
Yet.

And you cannot see
Where we, must needs, meet.

Where I as old
And you as young
Are one.

PART TWO

Behold beauty, behold horror
Behold joy, behold suffering.
In the eyes of the children,
And in the eyes of the sick
And starving.
In all who sleep.

Behold death
Indifferent to the pain
Incognizant of the moment.
Death, cold and sure.

Young man,
Take the edge off death
With life.

Before death takes the edge of life from you.

PART TWO

MONUMENTS, MONOLITHS, PYRAMIDS AND MEN
(1988, Age 22)

The winds do sweep
And the hours creep
Across the empty ruins.

While the sun casts transient shadows
Like the sand
That shifts in dunes.

Crumbled empty structures
Fragmented highway roads
Dry deserted farmlands
Desolate abodes.

Fractured concrete sidewalks
A static steeple bell
If a breeze should sway it
Who for would it knell?

Monuments and monoliths
Pyramids and men
They all stood for something
But why, what for, and when?

PART TWO

It is the greatest mystery
This vacant manifest
It all seems so pernicious
That none of it was blessed.

For who does claim
This scarred remain
So haunting, and so bleak?
That makes it seem
What happened here
Unnatural and freak.

PART TWO

THE DAY DEMURE
(1988, Age 22)

Why then should the day
Halt the night's advance,
Rape her of her mystery
And steal her romance?

And not a sudden, blatant death,
But gradual and sure.
So dies the night-impassioned,
In comes the day-demure.

Some say the nights for fools,
For lovers and for friends,
And day the executioner
Gives each its bitter end.

But there are many places,
Where light can't get inside,
And they provide the refuge
Where foolish lovers hide.

Sometime after sunset,
Though the setting disc still burns,
The mystery and romance
Stealthily returns.

PART TWO

Then foolish friends and lovers,
From hiding come to meet,
And arm and arm go dancing
Down the darkened city street.

They dance to desperation's song
Only foolish lovers hear.
For the crisp night air brings boldness,
And the darkness hides the fear.

And if the day should never come,
And darkness could prevail,
Two fools in love could with delight
Live out their fairy tale.

PART TWO

WARM WINDS
(1988, Age 22)

When warm winds blow
The darkened snow
Across
A troubled sky.

And here once grew
The things I knew
It seemed
Could never die.

All leveled low
From a fiery blow
That which was
So high.

Once iron now rust
Once flesh now dust
All that loved
The lie.

Deep in the wrath
Of the aftermath
Sad souls
Forever cry.

PART TWO

As warm winds blow
All that I know
Into
An angry sky.

PART TWO

TIME DRIFTER
(1988, Age 22)

A thousand deaths I've died in vain
Each one a mortal dream.
A thousand times I've felt the pain
Of the universal scheme.

A thousand times I've played the part
Of rules that fate doled out,
Gave a performance with all my heart
As if the final bout.

Like tumbleweed through centuries
I've drifted far and wide.
A generation I would seize
Then decades I would hide.

I'd play the soldier in a war
Or live a lover's life.
Live ten lives of leisure
Then live ten lives of strife.

And always I come back.
And damn, I'm here again.
New life, new prey, attack!
That's how it's always been.

PART TWO

This time will be the last
At least it will for me.
I'll leave it to the past
And maybe I'll be free.

PART TWO

FRAME IN TIME
(1989, Age 23)

A windswept grain of sand am I,
A timeless entity to spy…
Upon a frame in time.

What many things could drift my way,
What countless roles there are to play…
Within a frame in time.

A legend here forgotten there,
My destiny is anywhere; dancing…
Along the frames of time.

An apparition leaves no name,
Drifting so from frame to frame…
Through the frames of time.

And should some passion leave a trace,
The memory of a lovers face…
'Twas just a frame in time.

Like the sunshine that once shone,
And lit the days of nights now gone…
So pass the frames of time.

PART TWO

The rays that warmed your tender skin
Will never pass this way again...
Lost is a frame in time.

But here today and gone tomorrow
Is not the catalyst of sorrow...
'Tis but a frame in time.

And if it happens that one day
I should chance to drift your way,
Perhaps you'll be the one to say,
Leave with me without delay...
Beyond the frames of time.

PART TWO

CAN YOU HEAR?
(1989, Age 23)

Illusion my son,
I thought you had heard?
Behind all the fancy façade
Is the Word.

Always your guide, your friend,
And your God.
Why does our bond now
Appear as so odd?

For I know when your ears
Heard nothing at all,
The sounds of the Lord
Were your beckon and call.

PART TWO

TOO BUSY DYING
(1989, Age 23)

The weeds of grass
Through earth's demise
Shall cover our
Bewildered eyes.

As we
Like hungry alter boys
Shall offer up
Our precious joys.

For sorrow, sin,
Despair, and grief;
To wait for sleep
And then relief.

Too busy dying
A thousand deaths,
We breathe of life
In shallow breaths.

What we destroy
Time cannot mend
Loss befriends
The bitter end.

PART TWO

The spark that prompted
Our first breath
Shall none the wiser
Leave at death.

And shake its head
In disarray
How humans can
Themselves betray.

PART TWO

PEACE
(1989, Age 23)

An open starry night
Brings emptiness to sight

And taunts tormented souls
To seek release

From bondage, pain and strife
From death, and maybe life

So sing the many souls
That cry for peace.

PART TWO

I AM
(1990, Age 24)

Devoid do I come unto The Creator
Empty of me...
My fears
My hopes
My dreams
My desires—
All wayside.

And I am nameless and pure
Cleansed of the knowledge
And master of its curse.

I beckon to the Christ
As a babe to a new day
And I am filled
Never denied.

And the love
And the beauty
And the wisdom
Are mine, and remain eternally here...

PART TWO

For
The nameless
The innocent
The loving
And the pure.

For here in heaven,
There is no doubt,
I am.

PART TWO

FREEDOM
(1990, Age 24)

I was gifted freedom wings,
And on my breath did freedom sing.

And as I flew to paradise,
My freedom songs did then suffice.

I flew swift and I flew high,
Engaged the love that doesn't die.

Wrapped myself in Godly peace,
It seemed to me would never cease.

Descended I then to the earth,
To chosen place, and chosen birth.

Took myself the fleshly cloak,
That God does give, and then revoke.

Gone were my precious freedom wings,
A mother's breast in trade to cling.

And freedom songs as soft as silk,
Now a cry for mother's milk.

PART TWO

Flew I once over this land I've trod,
Now closer to apes then I am to God.

Born of the water we feel the pain
Of the veil of darkness we grow to disdain.

But through the terror, the chaos, and strain,
We are born of the spirit and fly free again.

PART TWO

POOR MAN'S SON
(1990, Age 24)

When I was a child
With thoughts so free,
My father grabbed me tight saying,
"Son you'll see…

The winter's too cold,
And the summer gets hot,
And there ain't enough gold
In the leprechaun's pot."

I said to my father,

"Well don't chain me.
I'm a poor man's son—
Just let me be…

I'm a poor man's son,
Best let me be."

PART TWO

NOT YET
(1991, Age 25)

My faith is not yet alive.

It does not burn with passion
Like the fire that consumes its fuel.

It does not move in freedom
Like the roaring stream
That flows not for purpose,
But of necessity.

I cannot let go of the lie,
Because I am weak.

I cannot cling to the lie,
Because I am afraid.

I am a coward
And a fool.

And I thank God for my darkness,
Though I hate it so.

Because I will bring light to it.

PART TWO

And love all those who suffer by it.

And glorify the Light that delivered me from it.

Else I shall never have truly lived.

PART TWO

THE LOVER
(1991, Age 25)

I am brought to the brink of my experience,
To the endless oscillations of dark and light.
I am as empty as the wind,
Yet as full as the laws that govern and create it.

I am bound and tortured
To the threshold of my tolerance.
And yet, I am more free
Than the notion of freedom could ever know.

I am finite when my infinite nature ponders.
I am the elements of wholeness,
Like the moments that comprise a sunset.

I am flesh and spirit immersed in God,
Lost in the rapture of this perfect mystery
I cannot fathom.

I am the lover,
Which is the gift and solace of human beings,
Conqueror of dark and light,
And common key to the heart of God.

Part Three

1992 to 1999

(Ages 26 to 33)

PART THREE

PART THREE PRELUDE

I think at some point in our lives we look out at the condition of the world and begin to see both horror and beauty more deeply than ever before; we feel both pain and splendor in more intensified ways. But do we really slow down long enough to allow those polarities to take us apart and put us back together again?

Throughout Part Three, Robert continues his exploration of emotional textures, without pulling away from what he finds. I so appreciate the raw honesty in his writings, because I know that it arises through poems written privately and that were never intended for the public eye. Inside these ruminations he allows himself to be messy and feel all the irregularities of life without filter or cushion. He isn't concerned about neatly painting inside the lines of the canvas, but rather; he throws paint all over the room in a fit of passion, unconcerned about the final outcome. Despite this wild and unabashed quality of writing, the outcome is unintentionally *extraordinary*.

I find it inspiring how he allows for the full scope of our existence to come alive within his experience without contraction. Because of this staying power, he gradually comes to rest deeper in himself. This gradual hard-earned spaciousness begins to cultivate room for the organic qualities of tenderness, compassion and love to move generously through him.

PART THREE

MESSAGE
(1992, Age 26)

So many men have trodden shores
Of struggle and despair.
Some were left amidst the strife
And died not knowing where.

Some men damned the trodden shore
And cursed the wretched toil.
So earths extremes tortured there dreams
And reclaimed the bitter soil.

Some men craved the pleasures
Of a soft and soothing shore,
And gave not thought of the toiling lot
And died only wanting more.

Then came a man upon the sand
As never was before,
Who loved all things from peasants to kings
And knowing what life was for.

A message clear was spoken here
Some two thousand years ago,
To God you must give your life so to live
And your soul that it might grow.

PART THREE

CHAINS OF FIRE
(1992, Age 26)

Man would chain a sunrise
So it could rise no higher.
Horizon bound forevermore,
Like God in chains of fire.

The wish of men since time began
To quell and tame desire.
Clip the wings of passion's flight,
Put love in chains of fire.

Stolen dreams to ridicule
Relentless is the liar.
Blindfolds on the piercing eyes
Of truth in chains of fire.

And I condemn this travesty
Which fuels all my ire.
A world that stole my heart and bound,
My soul in chains of fire.

PART THREE

DARKNESS
(1992, Age 26)

It's hard to say
That I'm ok
That I deserve
Another day.

For what I've done
And what I've thought
With all the pain and suffering
I've wrought.

That I could receive
Or truly give
Love myself
And try to live.

From the halls of heaven
Forever barred
These wounds of sin
That leave me scarred.

Remind me
Of the dark inside
And the innocence
I put aside.

PART THREE

But...

If I ever believe
This lie complete
I'll drop my pen
And accept defeat.

PART THREE

THE TIMES WE LIVE IN
(1992, Age 26)

There is no denying
The times we live in.
The embarrassing slothfulness of it.

There are no heroes
In the game rooms.
No courage in the lounges.

Everywhere it seems, an empty, hollow, rhetoric.
The scant talk of the half-dead,
And the asleep.

What actual trials may arise
Are just a slap to the face of the lobotomized.
We are the worst in history.

The decadence of Babylon,
The lust of Gomorrah,
The arrogance of The Third Reich,
And the fall of Rome
All rolled into one stinking dung heap.

We may as well piss
On the graves of the great ones,
And smear feces on their headstones.

PART THREE

We inherit a liberty that has emerged
From the effort, blood and sweat of real courage,
And masturbate out of boredom with our free time.

Our most profound daily act
Is mopping up the semen
From off our fat white bellies.

We have failed to distill wisdom out of experience
Belching instead the substance of shadows.

To die in your sleep is the preferred method
Of expiration for today's man.

Need I say more?

PART THREE

LOVE THAT IS FIRE
(1992, Age 26)

A summer sun sets
On a warm June eve
As the games wind down
And the children leave.

Off to our houses
We abandon the streets
Farewells and laughter
And scampering feet.

Yet we are the daughters
And sons of the past,
Frightened of the very shadows
We cast.

We have learned fear
And we have learned hate,
Let all that is weak in us
Determine our fate.

We seek affections
To make us secure
Not the love that is fire
Distilling us pure.

PART THREE

We are children
Who want to be free,
But given no more
Than this dark legacy.

When will it stop?
When will we see?
Until we learn love,
We can never be free.

PART THREE

VIOLATING THE INFINITE
(1992, Age 26)

Better to stand naked against abomination.

> For Love is glorified most
> In its deepest violations…

> In as much as space
> Could violate the infinite.

PART THREE

PLUCKED
(1993, Age 27)

Once I stopped and pondered
Upon a mountain peak
Gazing down at valley lights,
Both dazzling and bleak.

I saw it was a city
This phosphorescent glow
I should have known if I were witty
But I did not want to know.

For something did so beckon
And I went for the shiny lure
I'll try it out I reckon
Careless and unsure.

So much into a vacuum
This molecule was sucked
As the death wish sealed its doom
From sanctuary plucked.

And suddenly the night
Was shattered like a glass
Darkness cremated by the light,
Pavement burying grass.

PART THREE

Derelicts and drunks
Signs of disoriented life
Criminals and punks
Poverty and strife.

Exposed to greed and sin
I wished I could be free
I saw the mountain where I had been
And longed for sanctity.

Where is the exit to this maze
Of ignorance and pain
Over exposure to a glaze
Like fog upon my brain.

When I found the way out,
After 100 miles gone
It occurred to me to wonder
Why was I ever drawn?

PART THREE

ONCE MORE?
(1995, Age 29)

When I was a child
With thoughts free and wild
Life then to me was a game.

Hide and seek in the dark
A swing in the park
Are things that I'd play without shame.

If I could just do it again O' Lord
If I could just try it once more,
There I would stay and continue to play,
If I could just try it once more.

When I was a teen
So young, quick and lean
Life then to me was a sport.

I'd fend off the blows
Of the challengers throws
Defending myself like a fort.

If I could just do it again O' Lord
If I could just try it once more,
To be young and ambitious and sometimes malicious,
If I could just try it once more.

PART THREE

Young manhood was like
The first ride on a bike
It was raw, it was fresh, it was new.

But what life had to deal
Seemed all too real,
Yet I still had dreams to make true.

If I could just try it again O' Lord
If I could just try it once more
I wouldn't lose hope if they tightened the rope,
If I could just try it once more.

When adulthood came on
I felt like a pawn
In the middle of a big chess game.

In tangling with fate
I'd lost to checkmate,
And sent to my corner in shame.

If I could just try it again O' Lord
If I could just try it once more,
I'd live in the light instead of the fight,
If I could just try it once more.

PART THREE

Old age has set in
And I think where I've been
The trails I've blazed make me sigh.

And now I just talk
Of the paths I should walk
Cause I haven't the strength to try.

But if I could just try life again O' Lord
If I could just try it once more,
For I'm old and I'm sore and deaths at my door,
Please let me try it once more.

Life's generous lend
Has come to an end
Gone is the pain and the strife.

And after the fall
Isn't end at all,
Save for the end of life.

Please set me free of that life O' Lord
Don't throw me back in the pen,
With the spirit in me, forever, set free
Please do not chain it again.

PART THREE

CYCLE
(1995, Age 29)

Crispy, golden leaves of Autumn
Upon the winds of death will ride.

From branch to wind, a journey's end
And there upon the ground subside.

Peaceful is the cycle of life,
And relentless is her tide.

Such beauty is there in a death
Where no struggle is applied.

Blessed is the eye that sees
That nothing there has died.

PART THREE

EMPEROR OF THE GRAVE
(1996, Age 30)

To the West I speak
Voice to the wind,
Shall it carry?

You on your deathbed
Dying since you were born,
Never living.

Building an Empire
Out of a grave,
With gold you shall die.

All glory is yours
Proud West.

You have won the wars.
Spoils to the victor,
Long live
The Emperor of The Grave!

Put in your 80 years
West man,
And be gone!

PART THREE

Gone with your wants,
Your lusts,
Your desires,
Your ambitions.

Dead.
Dead with all else
That hinders life.

Oh yes, West Man
It is your right
To bask in the glory
Of an Emperors rule,
And die in the grave
That you dug
Like a fool.

And for what?

Behold West Man,
The meaningless cycle of
The Emperor of The Grave.

PART THREE

CONFLICT IS
(1996, Age 31)

Conflict is…

A dance that's done
Without musical host
Where partners embrace
The flesh of a ghost.

Where all that's felt
Or said, or done
Is a futile attempt to fight
Or to run.

Conflict is where you and I
Forget each other,
Give up
And die.

PART THREE

"OLOGY'S" AND "ISMS"
(1997, Age 31)

"Ology's" and "isms"
Have bombarded me in rhythms,
Since the day I first sat down
    In grammar school.

I've learned proof
And I've learned theory,
Postulated till quite weary.
Compiled stats until
They reached up to the roof.

Facts are all we're given,
    Dissecting life
    Instead of living.
   Tampering with truth
    Until it lies.

We'd rather play the sleuth
Than discover the one truth,
    That life itself
  Is right before our eyes.

PART THREE

NOTHING TO ANYONE
(1997, Age 31)

Some they call me son.
Some they call me lover.
Some they call me friend.
Some they call me brother.

Some would call me stranger.
Some don't even care
What anybody calls me
Or if I'm even there.

Set me free from these
Is my sole decree
For I am nothing to anyone
Just God and Love and Me.

PART THREE

I BURIED YOU
(The Death of Little Self)
(1998, Age 32)

I buried you
In this open coliseum
Where circling winds claw
At the indifferent dust above you.

The earth I broke
To bury you, moaned
The way soil laments
When forced to cover landfills.

Here the drama of your story has disappeared
With the last inch of your cold flesh
That I covered with this uneasy clay.

Your new worth
Is measured slowly now
In increments of decay.

I remember how
You pissed and spat your days
Upon the earth.
Consuming beauty, hoarding time.

PART THREE

But now, in decomposing
Your surrendered flesh
Finally gives without volition
In one final act
Of pathetic contrition.

I chose to bury you in this arena,
Where all your fury
Once garnered opinions
And blood money.

Where your unbridled passions
Whored themselves
Among the tormented appetites
Of invalid pretenders.

Already I smell the decay of you
Which began even before your death,
You gladiator of pettiness and pomp,
You Caesar of smoke and ash.

If you could only see
The empty seats that surround you here,
And feel the thickness
Of their utter disregard.

PART THREE

You may have shook the world
When you were in it,
But your closing act didn't sell one ticket.

And now even I, having met my obligations
Will turn away and leave you
To your mute soliloquy in death,
And depart this stadium of hollow spectacle forever.

To wander the streets
Like a mad twin brother,
Laughing without smiling,
Waiting for your ghost to come and haunt me
With those beloved echoes
Of passion and fury.

PART THREE

AS MEN
(1998, Age 32)

Today, for a moment
I saw beyond my brother's face,
And deep to within his heart.

How vulnerable,
How innocent,
How sensitive,
How precious was this place.
How unlike the show.
How unlike the man.

Underneath the personality,
Beyond the ego,
Deep, at the core of his humanness.
A newborn,
With big wondering eyes
Puts out his hand
In complete innocence.

And somehow
Speechless,
Asks for love
Because the man outside
Won't let any in.

PART THREE

And I know
That if I took that infant hand
And loved it,

The man outside would die.
And so I just stare back.

And my heart weeps.
And his heart weeps.

And as men,
We somehow feel ashamed,
That we do not truly give
Because we fail to truly receive...

And the pain is deep.

Yet even so,
As men,
We cannot cry.

PART THREE

DUSK TO DAWN
(1998, Age 32)

When light concedes to night
And twilight phases in
Silhouettes prevail
Where deeper forms had been.

While the myriad of colors
Of shapes and forms robust
Display themselves by day
At night are held in trust.

Till morning' dawn has broken
And smiles upon the land
Caressing it with sunlight
Like mothers gentle hand.

PART THREE

EULOGY OF A METROPOLIS
(1998, Age 32)

San Francisco is dead.
Its bustling people,
A futile pulse
In a rotting corpse.

Whatever grandeur that land had,
Whatever topography nature had sculpted,
Is now buried in concrete.

I've been to Golden Gate Park,
And know
That it is only
The mediocre offspring
Of a once great sire.

It stands there,
Encompassed in filth,
Shamefully cognizant
That it cannot compensate tragedy,
And weeps amid the decay.

PART THREE

San Francisco,
Where man has overcome all but himself.
Where dreams are as heavy laden
As fog through the gate.
And life is a forgotten song
That sings muffled
Under a suffocating blanket
Of concrete, steel, and human indifference.

PART THREE

ANOTHER STORM
(1998, Age 32)

Like the eye of the storm
My mind has subsided,
Acquiescently merging
With its source.

Thoughtless I am
Realizing my passive sovereignty.

Only vibration
Harmony, peace and bliss.

From the dregs of Maya
And the gross manifest
A lonely, frightened ego inquires
Am I enlightened?

In a flash I am body!
My world is again the finite.

I am again separate, alone, and empty.

PART THREE

MORNING PRAYER
(1998, Age 32)

I arise this day
Consecrated to life
And in love with the truth of it.

Of my own will
And in absolute freedom
I enter into it.

Seeking the glory of the God
That created it.

And the love of God
That sustains it.

PART THREE

IT DON'T MEAN NOTH'N
(1998, Age 32)

You want me to play the game
    Take a number
    Forget my name?
    It don't mean noth'n.

You want me to close my eyes
    Sell my soul
    And compromise?
    It don't mean noth'n.

You think I should need your world
    And march under
    Your flag unfurled?
    It don't mean noth'n.

Your seeds of fear don't grow in me
    You hate me
    Cause you know I'm free.
    It don't mean noth'n.

Your lives are desire and fear combined
    A religion
    I long since resigned.
    It don't mean noth'n.

PART THREE

Live the lie and die dismayed?
I'm sorry
That I ever played.
Cause man, it don't mean noth'n.

PART THREE

FOR REASONS LONG FORGOTTEN
(1998, Age 32)

Where well known the salt air
Twists, gusts, and swirls.
Dancing ageless since history itself
Kept time.

Among the ceaseless tides of surging
White foam and ocean sprays.
In the effervescent saline mists
Where daunting summer sun
Disperses its range of colors
For play and to flaunt it's spectacle.

Here, amid this pulsing womb
Of erosion and change,
The hands of men have fashioned
Links of iron
Attached to sea soaked posts
For some good reason
Long defunct.

And the forces have scaled and scarred,
Corroded and rusted,
Weathering hard
The once sacred integrity of these
Massive links of steel.

PART THREE

They droop in dying despair
And yet they remain;
More symbol than meaning,
More reflection than relevance.

Cold brittle metal
Clinging hopelessly to the bellies
Of water logged tree corpses,
Poised vertically like a soul-less scarecrow's
Futile defiance against the raging elements of life.

Impotent phantasms against
The silhouette of the day,
Waiting to be swallowed
By deeper tides and the blanket of night.

No screams.
No tears.
No horror.
Not even the peace of death.

Inert, inanimate, and silent.
In the face of the churning
Pandemonium of Great Mystery.
This hallow stand
Of empty station remains.

For reasons and purpose long, long, forgotten.

PART THREE

SKY POET
(1998, Age 32)

I was the walker of winds
I danced upon the earth
Heaven implored my freedom
Nature knew my mirth.

I swept across the deserts
I skipped across the seas
Caressed the mighty mountains
And frolicked through the trees.

Everywhere my soul did move
Nothing did I miss
Till suddenly I felt from you
A warm and tender kiss.

Now I hold your body
And stare into your eyes
And move inside your soul
Where this ground of love resides.

I once was a poet of the sky
Where no one knew my name,
Now my lover calls me
Home from whence I came.

PART THREE

WHERE DO YOU LIVE?
(1998, Age 32)

Where are the elders
And the warriors?

Where is the lean
Agile boy, hungry
For the game?

In our ignorance
We have
Deemed them obsolete.

If there are such guests
We cannot honor them here.

A pig herder's hut inside
The realm of the one True King
Is worth more,
Than a mansion outside.

PART THREE

UNKNOWN LOVER
(1999, Age 33)

I set my foundations upon the unknown.
Upon the bedrock of infinite mystery.

I breathe and exhale something into nothing.

I trust only Love.

Love only Faith.

Faith beyond sorrow.

Faith beyond joy.

Loyal to the unknown lover
Whom I can feel but never touch.
Whom I can trust but never know.

Still, my heart beats naked to the sun,
Only because love and grace conspire to sustain it,
While the raw fists of the physical world
Pound my soul till my faith is dazed and bleeding.

Part Four
2000 to 2018
(Ages 34 to 52)

PART FOUR

PART FOUR PRELUDE

Though much of the spirit of these later works has to do with the freedom that comes with years of cultivating a depth of surrender that I have yet to realize, it is profound to be an intimate witness to the living embodiment of it in my husband. From ages 35 to 52 Robert passes through an era of transformational surrender that it seems few ever attempt. The poetry during this period reflects a man who never dismisses his humanness no matter how ecstatic his epiphanies are, no matter how transcendent his state is. This is the magic of the man I married; a soul who never abandons his mortal nature in favor of the deeply mystical reveries he has such intimate association with. His poetry now has distinctly graduated to the look and feel of the sage. His words reflect a surrender that seems to melt his essence— all while fiercely holding to a Renaissance ministry that blends warrior, prophet, poet, storyteller and philosopher all into one epic personality. Robert caps this exquisite chapter of his life with the ferocious "Lion Heart,"—written while I was finishing this book—letting us know that for him the journey continues with an honestly-earned tenderness that I see him demonstrate daily in our lives together.

PART FOUR

MY NAKED HEART
(2000, Age 34)

In some foolish fit of passion
I glared toward the heavens
And asked to feel life fully.

And the Gods granted my longing
So that now
There is nothing left but my heart
Beating blood red
In the heat of the day
And the cold of the night.

All else having been splintered
And fractured off
By the razor sharp chisel of human experience.

Now my naked heart
Is all I have to offer death.

PART FOUR

RISING TIDE
(2000, Age 34)

The world of men rushes by me
In ordered images.

Frame by frame I feel
The human movement
Imposing it's broken pieces.

It spreads like a disease
Of desperation across
These lands.

Hating and fearing what
Sustains it.

As if on a sand bar
Soon to be engulfed
By the rising tide.

PART FOUR

THE JOURNEY FOREVER
(2001, Age 35)

A single step young lord
Is what I ask of thee.

Not to falter
Not to stride
Not to hurdle
Not to sprint
Not to stumble

A single step young lord
Is what I ask of thee.

I ask for ground in inches
I offer The Journey Forever.
Not in recompense for steps.
Yet even so…

A single step young lord
Is what I ask of thee.

PART FOUR

GHOST TOWN
(2002, Age 36)

I find about a ghost town
Nothing sad or void.
Nothing lost forever,
No Camelot destroyed.

I find moreover a peacefulness,
A silent majesty,
That's quelled the viscous movement
Of the human travesty.

Has laughed at human pettiness
And buried greed's ambition.
Disregarded all the fervor
Of the church's holy mission.

Has watched the hearty miners
As they came and as they went
Watched their riches squandered
On prostitutes and rent.

The empty towns are monuments
To man and all his pains.

PART FOUR

Before the men there was a peace.
Man's gone,
That peace remains.

PART FOUR

HOME
(2002, Age 36)

Slender are the days
Between sunrise and sunset.
Narrow and deep
Like the gorge of ages.

Elusive like primordial dust
Scattered here,
Convergent there.

Eyes fail to see so small
Or to gaze so distant
As to see the circle
Complete itself.

Like dust and seeds
Aloft on breezes
Faint recollections of forever
Permeate our journey
And visit in our dreams.

We recall a home
Somehow related,
In some way connected.
A home that gives
Birth to slender days.

PART FOUR

The home that is heard
In the deepest, stillest
Most silent part of the day.
Where the heart of creation
Moves love through the circle.

Home, for which we long.
Home, that keeps us lovingly at bay,
So that we may exist slightly apart
Just enough to know
And embrace one another.

PART FOUR

SCATTERED MATTER
(2002, Age 36)

Lo, I am reconciled to death,
She is my lover.

She loves divorce
But she is just a mistress to me.

So explode my brain and all its thoughts.
Yet still I will remain
To laugh at so much scattered matter.

I knew you when you dreamt
Of life.

But now I'd wake you up.

PART FOUR

WOKEN UP
(2002, Age 36)

What was that wild segue into positioned perception?
That odd foray into object relations.

What was that strange condensation of consciousness about?
That curious subjectivity that follows the carnal kiss of mortality.

Whatever it was that dreamed itself into that reverie,
Has finally woken up,
And emptied itself
Of all singularity.

PART FOUR

MY TEACHER
(2002, Age 36)

My teacher defeats me.
Her grace demonstrates
My imperfection.
She knows her opponent.
But she knows no opposition.

Until now,
Even in defeat, I have never surrendered.
But to this one,
I finally kneel.

My love is exceeding for this slayer
Of ignorance, who laughs with her
Blade running through my throat saying,
"Let the dead bury the dead—
Who is this that lives still?"

PART FOUR

I SHALL FIGHT NO MORE FOREVER
(2002, Age 36)

I shall fight no more forever
Spoke the warrior today,
And he lay down all his weapons
Turned his back and walked away.

He ends the war of millions
And begins the war of one.
No armor will protect him
For no sorrows will he shun.

With no battle ground to fight upon
He'll die without delay.
I fight no more forever
Spoke the warrior today.

I shall stir no more forever
Spoke the water from the sea.
My waves shall break no more upon
The shores of Galilee.

My tides shall know the stillness
Of the deepest darkest night,
And the heavy silence of my depths
Shall be my sole delight.

PART FOUR

No, not the slightest current
May surge again in me.
I shall stir no more forever
Spoke the water to the sea.

I shall blow no more forever
Spoke the wind up in the sky.
No more caress the things I love
Erode what I defy.

Silence in the firmament
Shall be my only creed.
Stillness between the sky and earth
To satisfy my need.

I will not carry seed aloft
With spring I won't comply.
I shall blow no more forever
Spoke the wind up in the sky.

I shall shine no more forever
Spoke the sun in heaven's womb.
Send the cold and fearful darkness
Of an apocalyptic doom.

PART FOUR

Upon the face of all I love
The pickled stares of death.
A requiem of hollow screams
From frozen static breath.

I shall bury all my children
In a dark and icy tomb.
I shall shine no more forever
Spoke the sun in heaven's womb.

PART FOUR

HAWK FEATHER
(2002, Age 36)

Like all movements of Power and Magic
I will cross your path just then...

Like all movements, I become change.
I will not be held to form,
But must be received on the cusp
Of timelessness as essence.

Once I was that which
In communion with my kind
Held aloft the wings of freedom,
And it's corporeal agent
The hawk spirit.

I did then beat against the air of the moment
And gained lift;
Even amid the stillest and thinnest air.
For I was created to soar.
It is my nature.

In flight, my journey is ever rediscovered
And unfolds toward perfect destination
To which I never arrive.

PART FOUR

My message is as brief as my form.
But my meaning is forever.

PART FOUR

THRESHOLD
(2002, Age 36)

Standing upon the threshold of all we know
Gazing out into that....
That which must be,
Yet now, this moment
Is not of us.

Upon that threshold we stand.
A moment's hesitation,
A mortal eternity.

And again,
When the ominous face of
Transition appears...
We hesitate.

And we realize
That the security of what
We leave behind
Is the only real bondage
To the threshold.

PART FOUR

If I take, I leave behind.
But what I leave I hope to find.
What's on the other side?
And is it fair
One cannot share
What thresholds do divide?

A last great doubt?
The final bout?
Transition claims no fight.
Take your mark.
Seek out the dark.
The fledgling must take flight.

PART FOUR

ENEMY, MY ENEMY
(2002, Age 36)

Enemy my enemy
Let me eat with appreciation from your table.

Let me share a sunset
Looking out through your home's window.

Let me comfort your children
Through strange sounds in the night.

Let me anoint the forehead of your mother
With oil and gratitude.

Let me humbly walk a while in your shoes
And follow the trail of your ancestor's tears.

Let me embrace you, my enemy.

And like a sacred bath
Let love wash our pain
With the very blood
That has been spilt between our fathers.

And let us weep deeply
My adversarial brother.

PART FOUR

Let us mourn together this tragic misunderstanding,
That you and I could have chosen to believe
That the other ever wanted more than love.

PART FOUR

SHADOWS AND SHALLOW BREATHS
(2004, Age 38)

Shadows and shallow breaths
Lives lived faintly through
Dreamy deaths.

Begging to see
With eyes shut tight,
Deliverance from
Our chosen night.

Soggy wills
On misty days,
Huddled in the alleyways.

Disparate from
The common drone,
Waiting for the light
Alone.

PART FOUR

THIS DREAM
(2004, Age 38)

What is it to be a tear?
To cherish the very sorrow
That was your father.
To love the maternal grief
That gave you your watery birth.

In distinction, I have
Tasted the dream of
You and I.

And I have known you
In the very breath of my days
Inside and outside.
All at once distinct,
But inseparable.

When you laughed
It echoed in my soul.

And when you cried
I spread my heart
Across Creation
So no part of you
Would ever feel
You were alone.

PART FOUR

And now
I have chosen
To drown.
Only to discover
That I am the water
That kills me as well.

And you and I
Have awakened
Outside birth and death
Opening our single heart
To one Presence, forever.

PART FOUR

REPEAT OFFENDER
(2004, Age 38)

No one lives on sidewalks or freeways.
Concrete is a means, never an end.

As if the eight ball loved the green felt
On it's way to the corner pocket.

Has our laden respiration
Forgotten that the wind is effortless?

Circles are the logos of repeat offenders.

The genius of the wheel…
Laughable to the hawk.

Our lives have become
Board games of madness,
Played inside stale walls
While apples grow ripe and juicy outside.

No talk of moment-to-moment miracles.
We're too busy researching
The antidote to madness.

PART FOUR

BEGUILING LOVER
(2005, Age 39)

You are a beguiling Lover.
You make me search for you
In the space between gold coins.

You insulate my suffering,
Adding feathers to my comfort.

You require that I recognize you
In the banal and mundane
While you dazzle my attention
With fathomless beauty.

In my dreams you whisper
That these opposites
Are just laughter in the void
Disguised as something.

You wait with still breath
For the homecoming
We dreamt of from the beginning.

PART FOUR

Shatter this vessel
Dissolve the gold
Evaporate the beauty
And impale my comfort
On the steel blade of your True Love.

Nothing else matters.

PART FOUR

MYSTERY
(2005, Age 39)

Somewhere in this land
There's a definite plan
That leads stray horses to water.
And if you listen clear
It's sure you will hear
The cries of our sons and our daughters.

When all the voices fade
From the languages made
To teach the earth's children survival.
Nothing will remain
Of the faces and the names
That prayed for desire's revival.

Nothing it is said
Can ever save the dead
When the dying see nothing but blindness.
Perhaps we all knew
This has always been true,
But no one was there to remind us.

PART FOUR

Endure the stark chill
Of the scientific skill
But remember the name of the Silence.
You must feel the sting
And the darkness it brings
As long as the world knows violence.

Oh, somewhere in this land
Is a trail in the sand
That disappears soon after travel.
When winds over dunes
Turn human wills to ruins
The mystery will surely unravel.

PART FOUR

NO THOUGHT
(2005, Age 39)

I came to know that I know nothing.
That there is no control.
No formula.
No ideology.
No thought,
Not even madness
To comfort.

What is comfort?
I am alone and separate.
So alone
That I would welcome a vacuum to surround me.

And then I am shattered.

And yet I remain.

What is shattered?
What is it that remains?

Truly,
What can we know more than a blade of grass?
What can we do more than love?

PART FOUR

FAITH
(2005, Age 39)

Before we think
We must apprehend faith.

Before we act
We must apprehend faith.

Before we live
We must apprehend faith.

True faith
Is the foundation of life.

For whatever is built,
Apart from it
Cannot stand in truth,
But illusions only.

And what stands in illusion
Cannot endure.

Life can proceed only from true faith.
All else is animated death.

PART FOUR

TETE-A-TETE
(2005, Age 39)

When first burst fourth the thrust
Of cosmic providence
I screamed between the atoms then
My Name.

And in the boundless black of space
I sculpted time,
And I warped the infinite.

Gravity was my notion
And I wove the cosmos with it.
I gathered dust and dreamt of forms.
I craved life and gave it force.
I had a notion
So I made humankind…

I sat one day,
Completely expanded
In the face of God.
Infinite mystery, utterly alone.

PART FOUR

I am as a man with a mirror,
Pondering the nature of his own reflection,
Immersed in the madness
Of his own duality.
A part to die,
A part to remain without context.

The zenith of a dream
Some force has dreamt.
A symphonic gesture of self-reverie.
The whole damn universe
The music of a composing God.

And the love that binds us all,
My only consolation.
My only truth.
My only life.

PART FOUR

BRING ME TO THE FIRES
(2006, Age 40)

Bring me to the fires!
Bring me to the fires cried the soul!
Fires that possess the flames
To burn what is not whole.

Bring me to the fires,
Let us spend the wicked fuel.
Let us consume the violence
On both sides of the duel.

Bring me to the fires
That burn the bone and tooth,
That devour every atom
Till nothing left but truth.

Burn me in the fires
Is my adamant request,
Till nothing there but love remains
In truth, I then can rest.

PART FOUR

MEANINGLESSNESS
(2006, Age 40)

I know now the secret peace of cloud wisps
And the passing fluidity in streams
Going nowhere.

Oh, the lie of destinations
And the seduction of meaning!
Who conjures that barren interpretation
Of the call to Presence?

Of cursing Gods and demons
And with exhausted hands
Hanging life out to dry on a clothesline of death.

Yet now the sweet cool breeze!
Gone are the delusions of the untouchable soul.
The healer does dance with disease.

And I see clearly that
Every effort I have made to control
Has been a desperate measure
Not to feel
The truth of meaninglessness.

PART FOUR

OUTSIDE MYSELF
(2006, Age 40)

One half step outside myself
I thought to prepare my mind for the execution

One version has it I was blindfolded and shot.
The other version, I delivered the bullet.
I remember the horror of both.
The horror even of smelling a rose
While one half step outside myself.

On the one hand I recall
Being a host to the hot metal
Ripping through the memory of my flesh
And all its prescribed DNA.

The madness of it all,
Wanting to hold on to something
To carry me through the event,
Even when my body couldn't.

The horror of partiality and incompleteness
As my last moments of awareness
Bled into the unknown.

PART FOUR

I wished for some split second
That I had befriended the very silence
I had run away from my whole life.
That if I had loved it then,
I could ease into it now
Without this terror, this awful divergence.

And then I was the shooter.

Again one half step outside myself
Feigning duty, and self-righteousness
Lost in a labyrinth of judgment,
My trigger finger hating its roots.

My will, flattening the soul.
Driving it deeper into concept,
Never again to feel the rapture
I once knew as a child.

When the world made no sense,
And my fingers
Never dreamt of acting on their own.

PART FOUR

LOVE COMPLETES ITSELF
(2007, Age 41)

What Light created loss without lack?
Grief without despair?

We take on this flesh
With all its horrific paradox.

To live God's desperate Dream;
To Touch Itself.

We flutter in the elements of this firmament
Where all we apprehend
Can, must, and will fall away.

Here we dream of a passionate peace
Only to have dawn break upon our bloodshot eyes
With violent new horizons.

We are deeper than the Gods
Because we have chosen to wrap ourselves in flesh,
And fall asleep in separateness.

We suffer the night
On this prodigal journey,
Mad with the ways in which love completes itself.

PART FOUR

We turned away
To give perfection the texture of flaw,
And to give Love,
Rhythm.

PART FOUR

HOC PRIMUM DEDITIONEM
(This Surrender First)
(2007, Age 41)

Nothing I ever had
Drew up on this silent respiration.

None of my worldly accumulated treasures
Ever yearned to be spent on annihilation.

In the stark bite of a snowy evening
I am no longer obese with the world.

And my tears swell and extrude
Revealing the wet mystery of my soul.

Oh solitude,
Devoted husband to silence,
Forgive my heavy days of confusion.

For I stand now,
Naked at the foot of the bed
With nothing to offer except what remains
After an honest day's labor
In service to the One True Queen.

PART FOUR

"This Surrender First"
Emblazoned on Her coat-of-arms,
She smiles, revealing nothing.
And yet I know all that is required.

If ever I loved at all,
It occurred under Her sovereignty.
Blindly loyal to the stunning mystery
Of Her thrown.

PART FOUR

I HAVE NEVER KNOWN
(2007, Age 41)

Bring in the new innocence.
Stained but clear.
Intelligent but humble.
Intimate but free.

Blind from omniscience.
Lone lover of the un-possess-able.
Mad with unreasonable passion.
Mother of her soul, father of his destination.

If I asked for the comfortable journey,
Could such vanity set the terms?

I have never known earthly wisdom
So wise as unknowing.
So foolish as to embrace
Annihilation in the belly of immortality.

I have never known a force such as love…
Common ground of God and man.
Sublime essence of forever.
Sole fabric of Creation,
Blind to consequences,
Divinely driven.

PART FOUR

Regard this human potential highly.
The sweet gesture of divine contemplation.
Outside and in all at once.
Stranger and lover,
Favorite marriage of the Cosmos.

Though I might in time grow grey
And wax rich in language,
I shall never name
Nor directly communicate,
That which I love most.
That which has never failed.

Only at times I failed
To know that it could not.

PART FOUR

TILL ONLY LOVE REMAINS
(2007, Age 41)

What a ghost I have been
Haunting this world for years.
Explaining sunsets,
Calculating the flow of streams.

Forgetting the sun.
Looking up only
When it rains.

I have lived my life between
Conceptual bookends:
Birth and death.

My weeping has been a shield,
Not a spear plunging to the depths
of my own soul.

Expensive laughter fallen
Heavy and twisted from my lips.
Words careen forth
Drunk with motive.

PART FOUR

My affection a drug only,
That seeks the heart of another
As host and shelter
Against my own reflection.

And my doing.....
Dear God, my doing has been
The noise I create to try to avoid
The dreaded stillness
Of my own true perfection.

And I am weary.

Weary of predicting the wind
Controlling the tides
And guessing at stars.

So now I discover what I am not,
Till only Love remains.

PART FOUR

WHAT IS THOUGHT?
(2007, Age 41)

Hollow metal drone;
the grinding gears of reason,
drowning out the symphony
of my heart.

Where breezes once swept oe'r
and sweet warmth of sun caressed,
the wall of intellect
intrudes, surrounds.

A soul that leapt
across chasms of time and nothingness
to bridge this moment to forever
seems sealed, like infinity
in a jar.

Small wonder,
a thought is.

So small as to wonder
why anyone would think at all
in the face of Being.

PART FOUR

Why build a hall of mirrors
to reflect only our own image
in a thousand distorted ways?

Without light,
a mirror is mute.

What is a thought
devoid of spirit?

It is wind
devoid of movement.
It is fire
devoid of heat.
It is seed
devoid of potential.
A shadow only,
that takes itself as substance.

PART FOUR

TONIGHT I MEET THE DRAGON
(2008, Age 42)

Tonight I meet the Dragon
And engage him in the main.
And he will assume such forms
As would drive a man insane.

But I will drop my armor
For nothing stops the fires.
And I will embrace the moment's truth
And know we both are liars.

I'll yield myself to adversaries
And terrors I once fought.
For where a dragon breathes his fire
I know that I am not.

PART FOUR

BELOVED
(2008, Age 42)

Days pass by in merciful expedience.
Never has time's loss been so welcome.

When days are numbers in between our reunion
And sunsets are dominoes falling to that end,
I feel you in the moments between the tick of the second hand
Like a thin pulse living under the skin.

You who touched me like no other
You who smiled like sun and dew over my eternal morning.

Sweet budding Goddess
Nothing shakes your presence.

When you return I am yours,
Devoted as I have been since you pointed to my heart
And gave it's measured rhythms
Meaning.

PART FOUR

A SOFTNESS ONCE
(2010, Age 44)

My ears had a softness once
That listened to the sounds
Behind the noise.

Ears that heard the secret mutterings
Of aspen tap roots.
And the eulogy of sunsets
Followed by the soliloquy of dawn.

Ears that could hear the childhood stories
Of ancient redwoods
Thundering between the laughter of epochs.

Ears that could hear the impulse to take flight
Or the meaning of a river turning this way or that.

Ears that heard the release of autumn
Whisper to the boldness of summer… "Let go."

Yes, my ears had a softness once.

PART FOUR

MY MOTHER'S SON
(2010, Age 44)

There is a pain in my mother's heart.
I see in her eyes,
I feel in her touch,
Now that I am a man.

It is the pain
That the sun must feel
For all the planets that emerged once from it
Spinning out there in the darkness alone.

Each one different
With it's own qualities;
Molten, gaseous, freezing, burning—
But all her offspring,
No longer to embrace
Within her hydrogen womb.

Maybe a subtle kiss of
Warm sunshine if they
Are close enough to feel it.
But that is all.

PART FOUR

And what of the planet
Which has left the solar system altogether?
Blasted far out of reach of the sun by sundry forces.
Out of the gravitational influence of its mother,
And deep into the night of space, alone.

No sunshine kisses.
No comforting orbits to look forward to.
Just an endless influence of cosmic phenomenon
Upon a venturing mass
Moving through the void and substance of mystery.

Deep in my aloneness
In every molecule of my body
Exists my worldly mother.

And deep in that quiet space
Her pain becomes my pain
Because I understand it.

To give up something you love so much,
To know you cannot possess
That which you hold dearest.
And the ecstatic suffering
Of caring more for another than yourself.

PART FOUR

All this I have realized
In that mysterious abyss of manhood.
Like a planet's celestial recollections
Of it's cosmic birthright.

This is the pain we embrace.
This is the sublime love we share.
This is the essence of humanness.

I am my mother's son.

PART FOUR

ONLY MOTHS
(2011, Age 45)

Only moths grope in the dark
At cheap imitations of the sun.

Pale and rudderless,
Hearing rumors about sunlit butterflies.
Arguing in black and white
About color saturated wings,
And the hues of daylight.

Silly moth,
You thought light could be had.
Captured in pieces
In the corners of darkness.

Even a child knows
Light delivers itself
In the morning upon waking.

PART FOUR

THE DREAMER
(2016, Age 50)

Lord knows what happens when we sleep.
How the wretched orphans of the dark
Come out to haunt our sheets.

Unwashed as they are,
With dark circles under their eyes
And mouths agape in horror.
How this world has forgotten them;
Or worse, seen and neglected them.

They stare into our trembling psyches,
And all our horrors are fulfilled.

We wake and our skin is slimy,
Wet with the perspiration from a darker world.
Our slumber-heavy eyes see morning light
And the familiarity of home,
But we feel stunned with the recent episode
Of a dreamy homelessness.

PART FOUR

We lie in the early sun
Somehow unable to move without guilt or fear.
Our mind stutters with rumors
And gossip of the unconscious,
Like socialites at a fancy brunch,
Making shadows out of shade.

Our slumber likes to burrow into moldy corners
And avoids the open spaces of our soul.
Why does the unconscious dig through dumpsters,
Looking for scraps of food,
While fruit grows ripe and abundant all around?

We fell into the dream,
And forgot the Dreamer.

PART FOUR

I FOLLOWED YOU…
(2016, Age 51)

Through the sounds of desperate pleadings
Transiting thin walls,
And the postured betrayals of family.

Through nameless homes and fleeting beds
I cannot even remember waking up in,

I followed you…

Through the cyclic revolving of friendship-ghosts,
And the dry bosom of vulgar fraternal affections.

Through the huddled, creeping disaffect of youth,
And the tattered, crippled legions
Of teachers, counselors and coaches,

I followed you.

Through the flat, inert wanderings of rudderless dreams;
Meandering traction-less, without the weight of wisdom.

Through soulless labor,
And the savagely meaningless hours
Spent serving the scripted protocols of avarice,

PART FOUR

I followed you.

Through unreasonable desires,
And controversial passions
That burned more calories than I ever consumed.

Through numerous, quiet failures so pathetic,
No one even noticed them but me.

I followed you…

Through fancy romance and grinding companionship
That no one ever woke up from.

Through the black and still solitary hours
Without ceiling and without floor,

I followed you…

Through the weight of doubt, and despair,
And darkness so heavy
It pressed the very fluid of surrender from my flesh
From which I grudgingly drank, and finally saw…

You followed me.

PART FOUR

LEGEND
(2016, Age 51)

There is a tender dewdrop inside me,
Clinging to a blade of grass,
Horrified at existence.

There is a drying yellow leaf inside me,
Weary of holding on to this creaking old branch
In the autumn wind.

There is a fading ember from a once great fire in me,
Quietly releasing its final glow into the darkness,
Becoming only trails of soft smoke before it all ends.

I too am aghast.
I too know the stunning shock and overwhelm
Of living in this world.

And so like me,
Intimately, I know the deepest part of you.
That secret place that is appalled,
That contracts away from it all.
That terrified spot of pure reception
Trembling amid the spectacle of so much pain and suffering.

Like you, in that profound place
We cannot escape,

PART FOUR

I experience this life without filter,
Without protection.

Like you, I too want to control something
As if it were some antidote
To the venom of seeing too much in this world.

I would like to comfort you, if I were a liar,
To explain and justify it all with some satisfying rationale.
But if you trust me, know that there is none.
Know only that I am naked like you.

That when the storms came,
I too shook uncontrollably from the chill of it all.
That when the dear suffered and died,
Witnessing it, I broke open even deeper inside.
Yes, I too knew this world till it shattered me.

It was then that I stopped,
And being still,
Was placid amid the tempest toss.
Where I, as you, dissolve where Silence is.

That place is where we meet again
And remember as One,
That for every tender dewdrop,
This quality of peace will always be legend.

PART FOUR

NO ONE HIDES
(2018, Age 52)

In that hour I saw that it came for me
But not as a light in the darkness
But as the darkness itself.

It asked me where I thought I was hiding?
As if I had conjured refuge
From my own breath.

I trembled before that Presence,
Because I had fed on lies.

Under its gaze I tried to cover my nakedness.
I felt a stark aloneness bite to the bone
The moment it found me cold and exhausted.

I had prayed for the exposure to end
Wished even that it never had began.
I felt horror at having been discovered;
About being the very nightmare I was sleeping through.

I knew waking could never bring salvation,
Because I would sleep again.
I was designed to sleep,
As surely as I was to dream.

PART FOUR

It was then I heard the Presence:

"Wherefore does the fetus hide in the womb?
I fed you this darkness through the cord in your belly,
As certain as I nourished your very existence.
You imagine my milk is poison now
Because your tongue has learned its preferences.

Go now toward the air and the light
Empty your mouth of this encompassing fluid
Cut the cord of amniotic darkness
And breathe.

Walk then.
Walk away from me and do not look back,
Till we meet again somehow in that place
Where no one hides, and no one is found."

PART FOUR

LION HEART
(2018, age 52)

I have been the king of beasts
Gorged I upon the hard earned feasts
Where muscle, bone, tooth and claw
Enforced the rule of nature's law.

My eyes under the noonday sun
Bore down upon the frightened one
Where I as predator did roam
And all that is my prey was home.

My roar once shattered youthful pride
The most foolish of them swept aside
Under the force of my intent
A will to challenge forever bent.

I walk alone upon this earth
And wonder what my kingdom's worth
Where I control as is my right
The burning days, but not the night.

For destiny is not complete
Where command forgoes what is discreet
And I have missed by God's decree
The sensitivity in me.

PART FOUR

The lion heart has now come clean
The power in my shoulders lean
Can kill no more without a tear
For all that nourishes is dear.

In this place that I once ruled
With all the blood forever pooled
I killed and fought without regard
That tenderness could be so hard.

PART FOUR

Afterword

Until I met Robert, my life had textures of unnaturalness that I found deeply troubling. This caused my rapport with others to feel akin to bathing in shallow puddles; I was never fully saturated with the nourishment that comes with giving and receiving at depth. I felt intensely alone, and not just physically so. When I speak of aloneness, I speak of a certain form of existential isolation. I sense there is an organic place inside all of us that is designed to operate in some fashion of meaningful connection to others—a place that yearns to be truly recognized and seen for what we are at heart. That of course, requires our own recognition of that noiseless place within ourselves.

When I first met Robert, I was just beginning to touch in and out of this enigmatic self-intimacy. I wanted to dance deeper with it, but I wasn't sure how. Robert was, and is a man who had done that work, and it showed—immediately. Because he had deliberately taken the course of his lifetime to ascertain his true nature, he was able to recognize mine from the moment we met. I don't think I have to tell you of the valuable import of this.

I could speak to you of a thousand ways in which I love him personally, but this piece, this capacity of his to be intimate with all the aspects of my existence, dramatically changed the course of my life.

At the heart of this little poetry book is a love story—if you had not already guessed. It is our love story of course, but the

PART FOUR

content of what it is pointing to is about the power and nature of love itself. Our partnership was bestowed upon my life at only 25 years of age, and that gift has confirmed to me that the depth and scope of relating to one another in this profound way is available to all of us.

If there's only one thing you take away from reading this book, I hope you find the inspiration to risk everything in order to discover yourself honestly, and completely. Look, listen and feel as deeply as you can for that intimacy, and like my husband, keep at it with a lion's heart, "Till Only Love Remains."

www.ingramcontent.com/pod-product-compliance
Lightning Source LLC
Chambersburg PA
CBHW020411080526
44584CB00014B/1279